Mezzo-Soprano/Belter Volume

THE SINGER'S MUSICAL THEATRE ANTHOLOGY

A collection of songs from the musical stage, categorized by voice type. The selections are presented in their authentic settings, excerpted from the original vocal scores.

Compiled and Edited by Richard Walters

Mark Carlstein and Milton Granger, Assistant Editors

ISBN 0-634-00975-3

HAL•LEONARD® CORPORATION

7777 W. BLUEMOUND RD. P.O. BOX 13819 MILWAUKEE, WI 53213

Visit Hal Leonard Online at
www.halleonard.com

Foreword

The lively and ongoing interest in musical theatre may appear to be ironic in an age seemingly ruled by the media. The movie musical is dead (thank goodness for video and those classic movie channels!), show music is rarely ever broadcast on radio, and hoping to see any musical theatre on television—except for old movies—is usually like waiting for Godot. In such a world it takes a little effort to acquire a taste for musical theatre and a knowledge of shows, though to the devoted *conoscenti* it hardly feels like effort. As Volume 3 of *The Singer's Musical Theatre Anthology* proves, there is an amazing heritage of theatre repertoire and a growing appetite for it among singers of all descriptions.

As in the first two volumes for each voice type of *The Singer's Musical Theatre Anthology*, the editions of almost all the songs have been created from the piano/conductor score (or vocal score) of a show, allowing a more authentic rendition than standard piano/vocal sheet music. Original keys have been preserved whenever possible; occasionally either the original performing key is not known, or I chose to alter it for specific reasons. Common issues faced in creating solo editions of theatre music are removing chorus parts, eliminating other characters' lines, creating or deleting repeats, wrestling with musical form, and finding appropriate beginnings and endings. My aim is to present a performable excerpt from the show that stands alone musically, though is true to its context.

Categorizing musical theatre selections by conventional voice type remains an unending challenge. I have tried to be conservative in my criteria, though I quickly point out to singers and teachers that there is no exact science to this. In comparison, opera fachs are far more definite. Many women have told me they use both the Soprano and Mezzo-Soprano/Belter volumes, depending on the kind of singing they want to do.

We label this volume Mezzo-Soprano/Belter to clearly signal that all the songs in this volume can be belted if that's your natural style of singing. Recent stage productions afforded some valuable additional theatre literature. The Cabaret songs written for the film and added to the stage score for the Broadway revival are here ("Mein Herr," "Maybe This Time"). The lovely ballad "A Change in Me" was added to *The Beauty and the Beast* on Broadway for Toni Braxton. (We chose to print a more universally singable range than her extremely low key.)

The theatre selections in this volume range from the comic to the dramatic, from famous numbers to wonderful discoveries, from the 1930s to 1998. Not every song is for every singer. I compile these collections with the needs of many different types of talent in mind. But everyone should be able to find more than a few terrific choices.

The twelve solo volumes of *The Singer's Musical Theatre Anthology* now total nearly 500 songs! The three volumes for any voice type offer a huge number of choices. The mezzo-soprano/belter books have 123 songs to choose from! Happy hunting.

Richard Walters, editor
August, 2000

THE SINGER'S MUSICAL THEATRE ANTHOLOGY

Mezzo-Soprano/Belter Volume 3

Contents

ABOUT THE SHOWS

The material in this section is by Stanley Green, Richard Walters, and Robert Viagas,
some of which was previously published elsewhere.

ANNIE GET YOUR GUN

MUSIC AND LYRICS: Irving Berlin
BOOK: Herbert and Dorothy Fields
DIRECTOR: Joshua Logan
CHOREOGRAPHER: Helen Tamiris
OPENED: 5/16/46, New York; a run of 1,147 performances

Irving Berlin's musical biography of scrappy gal sharpshooter Annie Oakley earned standing ovations for Broadway stars of two generations: the original, Ethel Merman, in the 1940s; and Bernadette Peters in the 1990s. The tune-packed musical traces Annie's rise from illiterate hillbilly to international marksmanship star as she's discovered and developed in the traveling "Buffalo Bill's Wild West Show." She falls hard for the show's chauvinistic male star, Frank Butler. And romance blossoms—right up until Annie begins to outshine Frank. Annie gets two chances to reflect poetically on romance. Comically, she observes the many reasons why "You Can't Get a Man With a Gun, with its yodeling-flavored chorus. On a dreamy, longing note, Annie tries to imagine what love will be like, in the ballad, "They Say It's Wonderful."

THE APPLE TREE

MUSIC: Jerry Bock
LYRICS: Sheldon Harnick
BOOK: Jerry Bock & Sheldon Harnick, with Jerome Coopersmith
DIRECTOR: Mike Nichols
CHOREOGRAPHERS: Herbert Ross, Lee Theodore
OPENED: 10/18/66, New York; a run of 463 performances

Here was a new concept for Broadway: one musical containing three separate one-act musicals, like Puccini's *Il Trittico* or Offenbach's *Tales of Hoffmann*. Though the stories in *The Apple Tree* have nothing in common and, in fact, could be played separately, they are tied together by interrelated musical themes and by the whimsical reference to the color brown. Act I is based on Mark Twain's "The Diary of Adam and Eve," and deals with the dawn of humanity and innocence. Act II is based on Frank R. Stockton's short story, "The Lady or the Tiger?," in which a warrior's fate, unresolved in the story, is determined by the choice of door he enters. Act III is based on Jules Feiffer's "Passionella," a uniquely American take on "Cinderella," in which a female chimney sweep fulfills her dream of becoming a glamorous movie star. In this last section, the heroine comically glories in the fact that she is, at last, "Gorgeous."

BEAUTY AND THE BEAST

MUSIC: Alan Menken
LYRICS: Howard Ashman and Tim Rice
BOOK: Linda Woolverton
DIRECTOR: Robert Jess Roth
CHOREOGRAPHER: Matt West
OPENED: 4/18/94, New York, still running as of 7/1/2000

Disney made its Broadway debut with a big-budget adaptation of its own, Oscar-nominated animated film musical. Like the classic fairy tale on which it is based, *Beauty and the Beast* tells the story of a witch who transforms a haughty prince into a fearsome Beast (and his retainers into household objects). Her spell can be broken only when the prince learns how to love, and how to inspire love. Lyricist Ashman died in 1991 just as the film was coming out. The stage score includes several trunk songs written for the film, but not used, plus five new songs with lyrics by Broadway veteran Rice. Headstrong young woman Belle discovers the Beast's castle after her father is captured and held prisoner there. She bravely offers to exchange herself for her father, and soon finds herself adopted by the various living clocks, teapots, candlesticks and cutlery who strive to matchmake their beastly boss and the eligible but understandably resistant maiden. In "A Change in Me," Belle realizes that her feelings for the increasingly gentlemanly Beast are beginning to soften. The song was added to the show mid-run when pop diva Toni Braxton played Belle.

CABARET

MUSIC: John Kander
LYRICS: Fred Ebb
BOOK: Joe Masteroff
DIRECTOR: Harold Prince
CHOREOGRAPHER: Ron Field
OPENED: 11/20/66, New York, for a run of 1,165 performances

This moody musical captures the morally corrupt world of Berlin's demimonde just as the Nazis were coming to power. American writer Cliff Bradshaw moves in with Sally Bowles, the hedonistic star singer at a seedy nightclub. Soon, he comes to see all of Germany through the dark lens of that increasingly menacing cabaret, which is ruled over by a ghostly Emcee. When Cliff dickers over the rent for his tiny apartment, the landlady shrugs and explains why such things no longer mean anything to her, in "So What?" That number was written as a pastiche of composer Kurt Weill, and was originated in *Cabaret* by Weill's real-life widow, Lotte Lenya. Two songs were added to the film version to build up the role of Sally for star Liza Minnelli. She gives a Dietrich-like come-on to men everywhere in "Mein Herr," and lets her cynicism slip for just a moment in the ballad "Maybe This Time." The songs were inserted into the stage version for the Tony-winning 1998 Broadway revival.

CHICAGO

MUSIC: John Kander
LYRICS: Fred Ebb
BOOK: Fred Ebb and Bob Fosse
DIRECTOR-CHOREOGRAPHER: Bob Fosse
OPENED: 6/3/75, New York, for a run of 872 performances

Based on Maureen Dallas Watkins' 1926 play *Roxie Hart* this tough, flint-hearted musical tells the story of Roxie (Gwen Verdon), a married chorus girl who kills her faithless lover. She manages to win release from prison through the histrionic efforts of razzle-dazzle lawyer Billy Flynn (Jerry Orbach), and ends up as a vaudeville headliner with another "scintillating sinner," Velma Kelly (Chita Rivera). This scathing indictment of American hucksterism, vulgarity and decadence may have been ahead of its time in its original 1975 production. It was also overshadowed by the opening of *A Chorus Line* the same season. But it came roaring back for a stylish, Tony-winning 1996 revival that has already run longer than the original. Gruff, corrupt prison matron Mama Morton has two chances to shine in song. In "When You're Good to Mama," she explains the jailhouse rules: inmates who want favors need to *do* favors. In the comic "Class," she laments the passing of good manners—when it's clear that she's scarcely better herself.

A CHORUS LINE

MUSIC: Marvin Hamlisch
LYRICS: Ed Kleban
BOOK: James Kirkwood and Nicholas Dante
DIRECTOR: Michael Bennett
CHOREOGRAPHER: Michael Bennett and Bob Avian
OPENED: 7/25/76, New York; a run of 6,137 performances

Until overtaken by *Cats*, this musical stood for years as the longest-running show in Broadway history. It also won numerous Tony Awards, including Best Musical, plus the Pulitzer Prize. The story is simple: seventeen dancers reveal their life stories as they audition and compete for eight chorus parts in an unnamed Broadway musical. The show concentrates on the joys and troubles of their childhood and teen years. Puerto Rican actress Priscilla Lopez stopped the show nightly with "Nothing," her comic/tragic account of how she survived an ogre of an acting teacher.

COMPANY

MUSIC AND LYRICS: Stephen Sondheim
BOOK: George Furth
DIRECTOR: Harold Prince
CHOREOGRAPHER: Michael Bennett
OPENED: 4/26/70, New York, a run of 706 performances

Company was the first of the Sondheim musicals to have been directed by Harold Prince, and more than any other musical, reflects America in the 1970s. The show is a plotless evening about five affluent couples living in a Manhattan apartment building, and their excessively protective feelings about a charming, but somewhat indifferent bachelor named Bobby. They want to fix him up and see him married—even though it's clear their own marriages are far from perfect. In the end he seems ready to take the plunge. Making a connection with another person, the show says, is key to happiness. The songs are often very sophisticated, expressing the ambivalent or caustic attitudes of fashionable New Yorkers of the time. The show's "eleven o'clock number" went to Elaine Stritch, as the boozy, savage older woman who makes a failed pass at Bobby. She lashes out in "The Ladies Who Lunch," an indictment of an entire class of women (which may include her) who have too much money, too much free time and not enough real life.

COWGIRLS

MUSIC AND LYRICS: Mary Murfitt
BOOK: Betsie Howie
DIRECTOR AND CHOREOGRAPHER: Eleanor Reissa
OPENED: 4/1/96, New York, for a run of 319 performances

This Off-Broadway spoof recreates the calamitous night the classical Coghill Trio gets booked to play at the grand opening of a country-western music hall. It seems the manager misread the name of their group as the "Cowgirls Trio." The three ladies are left to adapt their classical repertoire to the needs of the hootin' 'n' hollerin' clientele, and they do so *con brio*. "Don't Call Me Trailer Trash" is a comedy cry for respect. "Heads or Tails" is a lament about fate.

DO RE MI

MUSIC: Jule Styne
LYRICS: Betty Comden and Adolph Green
BOOK AND DIRECTION: Garson Kanin
CHOREOGRAPHERS: Marc Breaux and Deedee Wood
OPENED: 12/26/60, New York; a run of 400 performances

A wild satire on the ways in which the underworld muscled in on the jukebox business, *Do Re Mi* was adapted by Kanin from his own novel. With characters reminiscent of the raffish Runyonland denizens of *Guys and Dolls*, the show offered two of Broadway's top clowns of the era: Phil Silvers as a fast-talking would-be big shot, and Nancy Walker as his long-suffering spouse. Nathan Lane and Randy Graff starred in a 1999 "Encores!" revival of the show (recorded by DRG). Both Walker and Graff stopped the show with "Adventure," the wife's explanation of why she stays with her man through every nutty get-rich-quick scheme that never seems to get them rich.

FOLLIES

MUSIC AND LYRICS: Stephen Sondheim
BOOK: James Goldman
DIRECTOR: Harold Prince
CHOREOGRAPHER: Michael Bennett
OPENED: 4/4/71, New York, a run of 522 performances

Taking place at a reunion of former Ziegfeld Follies-type showgirls, the musical deals with the reality of life as contrasted with the unreality of the theatre. *Follies* explores this theme through the lives of two couples, the upper-class, unhappy, Phyllis and Benjamin Stone, and the middle-class, also unhappy, Sally and Buddy Plummer. *Follies* also shows us these four as they were in their idealistic, pre-marital youth. The young actors appear as ghosts to haunt their elder selves. Because the show is about the past, and told often in flashback, Sondheim styled his songs to evoke some of the theatre's great composers and lyricists of the past. One of Sondheim's great challenges in the show was to come up with a song that would express the ferocious conflict inside Phyllis, the chorus girl who becomes a society matron. The Broadway score uses "The Ballad of Lucy and Jessie" to describe the two warring women inside her. But two other songs have been written for that spot, and both have emerged to become singer's favorites. An early version of the song, "Uptown, Downtown," makes the conflict geographic. A later version, "Ah, But Underneath," replaced "Ballad" in the 1987 London production.

FOOTLOOSE

MUSIC: Tom Snow (additional songs by Eric Carmen, Sammy Hagar, Kenny Loggins and Jim Steinman)
LYRICS: Dean Pitchford
BOOK: Dean Pitchford and Walter Bobbie
DIRECTOR: Walter Bobbie
CHOREOGRAPHER: A.C. Ciulla
OPENED: 10/22/98, New York; still running as of 7/1/2000

Based on the hit 1984 film musical of the same title, *Footloose* tells the story of a tiny midwest town where dancing is illegal. It seems the son of town preacher Rev. Shaw Moore was killed in a car accident after a dance some years back, and, in the aftermath, Rev. Moore moved the town council to enact the ban. Enter town newcomer Ren McCormack, who quickly becomes a rebel with a cause: he works to overturn the ban even as he courts Rev. Moore's pretty daughter Ariel. Despite mixed reviews, the show quickly became a favorite with younger audiences, partly because of its subject matter, and partly because of the pervasive high-energy dancing that broke the town's ordinances left and right. Ren has gotta dance! Rev. Moore becomes so obsessed with Ren's defiance that he begins to tyrannize Ariel. Ariel's mom, Vi, steps in to say she's having trouble recognizing the man they all once loved, in the song "Can You Find It in Your Heart?"

7

FUNNY GIRL

MUSIC: Jule Styne
LYRICS: Bob Merrill
BOOK: Isobel Lennart
DIRECTION: Garson Kanin and Jerome Robbins
CHOREOGRAPHERS: Marc Breaux and Deedee Wood
OPENED: 3/26/64, New York; a run of 1,348 performances

The funny girl of the title refers to Fanny Brice, one of Broadway's legendary clowns. Her story, told mostly in flashback, covers her discovery by impresario Florenz Ziegfeld, her triumphs in the Ziegfeld Follies, her stormy marriage to smooth-talking con man Nick Arnstein, and the breakup of the couple after Nick has served time for stock swindling. Film producer Ray Stark, Miss Brice's son-in-law, had long wanted to make a movie based on the Fanny Brice story, but the original screenplay convinced him that it should first be done on the stage. At one time or another Mary Martin, Carol Burnett and Anne Bancroft were announced for the leading role, but the assignment went to 22-year-old Barbra Streisand, whose only other Broadway experience had been in a supporting part in *I Can Get It for You Wholesale*. However, Streisand, through performances in clubs and on television and on record, had already begun her fast ascent to stardom. She was hardly an unknown on the opening night of *Funny Girl*. The 1968 movie version, directed by William Wyler and Herbert Ross, was Miss Streisand's auspicious film debut. In Act I, faced with uncomplimentary revelations about Nick, Fanny flings them aside with "Don't Rain on My Parade," an anthem about her determination to grab for happiness, whatever the cost.

GIRL CRAZY

MUSIC: George Gershwin
LYRICS: Ira Gershwin
BOOK: Guy Bolton and John McGowan
DIRECTOR: Alexander Leftwich
CHOREOGRAPHER: George Hale
OPENED: 10/14/30, New York, a run of 272 performances

Most theatregoers around today associate the songs of the 1930 *Girl Crazy* with the 1992 rewrite, *Crazy for You*. Certain key themes—e.g. the fish-out-of water comedy of a New Yorker stuck in an Arizona backwater—remain, but the characters and plot turns were quite different. In a role originally written for comedian Bert Lahr, Willie Howard played a New York taxi driver who takes a fare to Custerville, AZ and winds up as sheriff—and wins a tough, pretty cowgirl as his sweetheart. In a role originated by 19-year-old dancer Ginger Rogers, the cowgirl got to sing the romantic Gershwin ballads, particularly the wistful "But Not for Me," in which she feels left out as seemingly everyone else in the world finds love.

GYPSY

MUSIC: Jule Styne
LYRICS: Stephen Sondheim
BOOK: Arthur Laurents
DIRECTOR AND CHOREOGRAPHER: Jerome Robbins
OPENED: 5/21/59, New York, a run of 702 performances

Written for Ethel Merman, who gave the performance of her career as Gypsy Rose Lee's ruthless, domineering mother, *Gypsy* is one of the great scores in the mature musical comedy tradition. The idea for the musical began with producer David Merrick, who needed to read only one chapter in Miss Lee's autobiography to convince him of its stage potential. Originally, Stephen Sondheim was to have supplied the music as well as the lyrics, but Miss Merman, who had just come from a lukewarm production on Broadway, wanted the more experienced Jule Styne. In the story, Mama Rose is determined to escape from her humdrum life by pushing the vaudeville career of her daughter June. After June runs away to get married, Mama focuses all her attention on her other daughter the previously neglected Louise. She bucks up her dubious daughter and appalled boyfriend in the landmark Broadway anthem "Everything's Coming Up Roses." As vaudeville declines, so does their fortunes, until an accidental booking at a burlesque theatre, and Louise's ad-libbed striptease, turns Louise into a star—the legendary Gypsy Rose Lee. Rose achieves a version of her dream, but suffers a breakdown when she realizes that she is no longer needed in her daughter's career ("Rose's Turn"). Several major stars have played Mama Rose. Rosalind Russell won the role in the 1962 film. Angela Lansbury toplined a successful mid-1970s revival in London and New York in the mid-1970s. Tyne Daly gave the role a new spin in 1989. Bette Midler brought the show to a wider audience in a mid-1990s TV adaptation.

I CAN GET IT FOR YOU WHOLESALE

MUSIC AND LYRICS: Harold Rome
BOOK: Jerome Weidman
DIRECTOR: Abe Burrows
CHOREOGRAPHER: Herbert Ross
OPENED: 3/22/62, New York; a run of 300 performances

Harry Bogen, the leading character in *I Can Get It for You Wholesale*, is an unscrupulous conniver who uses and misuses people on his way to the top. Adapted by Jerome Weidman from his own best-selling novel, the musical also helped two real-life young people on their way to the top: Elliott Gould, who played Harry, and his future wife Barbra Streisand, who played the overworked, unappreciated Miss Marmelstein. She sings about her life of rejection, and her desire to be called anything else in the world but "Miss Marmelstein." The production is set in New York's Garment District in the 1930s, where Harry rises in the business world through a series of shady deals, until he finally outsmarts himself. At the end, though, there is a hint of redemption when he gets a new job and his estranged sweetheart comes back to him.

I LOVE YOU, YOU'RE PERFECT, NOW CHANGE

MUSIC: Jimmy Roberts
LYRICS AND BOOK: Joe DiPietro
DIRECTOR: Joel Bishoff
OPENED: 8/1/95, New York; still running as of 02/01/00

This sleeper hit Off-Broadway revue turns a satirical eye on the whole messy process of being single, dating, finding romance, picking a mate, marrying, having children, having affairs, trying to rekindle the spark in marriage, etc. Though simple in its conception, the show truly found its niche as a good "date" musical, sailing past 1400 performances as of New Year 2000, and seeing productions in cities around the world. "Always a Bridesmaid" is a country-flavored comic lament from a woman who has worn more hideous bridesmaid dresses at more friends' and relatives' nuptials than she cares to remember.

IS THERE LIFE AFTER HIGH SCHOOL?

MUSIC AND LYRICS: Craig Carnelia
BOOK: Jeffrey Kindley
DIRECTOR/CHOREOGRAPHER: Robert Nigro
OPENED: 5/7/82, New York; for a run of 12 performances

Based on a 1976 book of the same title, the revue-like *Is There Life After High School?* introduces us to a group of grownups who relive with nostalgia and horror the agonies and ecstasies of their high school years. In the slow, contemplative "Nothing Really Happened," the women remember the night of their first real romantic moment—or was it?

JEKYLL & HYDE

MUSIC: Frank Wildhorn
LYRICS AND BOOK: Leslie Bricusse
DIRECTOR: Robin Phillips
CHOREOGRAPHER: Joey Pizzi
OPENED: 4/28/97, New York; still running as of 7/1/2000

Based on Robert Louis Stevenson's 1886 novella, *Dr. Jekyll and Mr. Hyde*, this show took nearly a decade to arrive on Broadway. However, the first full score by pop composer Frank Wildhorn was already familiar to most lovers of musical theatre from two widely circulated concept albums. These proved especially popular among professional skaters for the background music of their programs. A North American tour also helped make the show familiar to most of the rest of America before arriving in New York. As in the Stevenson book, a well-meaning scientist, Dr. Henry Jekyll, invents a potion that separates the noble side of man's nature from the evil, bestial side. Using himself as guinea pig, Jekyll soon finds he has unleashed an uncontrollable monster, Mr. Hyde, who cuts a murderous swath through London. Two women in his life help emphasize this difference: Jekyll's sweet innocent fiancée, Emma; and Hyde's scarlet-woman lover, Lucy. Injured by a rough customer, Lucy finds herself being treated by the gentle Dr. Jekyll, and she fantasizes about a relationship with him in "Someone Like You." Later, after she becomes entangled with Mr. Hyde, she contemplates escape to "A New Life."

LEAVE IT TO ME

MUSIC AND LYRICS: Cole Porter
BOOK: Bella and Sam Spewack
DIRECTOR: Samuel Spewack
CHOREOGRAPHER: Robert Alton
OPENED: 11/9/38, New York; a run of 291 performances

With a book loosely related to their own play, *Clear All Wires*, Bella and Sam Spewack came up with a spoof of Communism and U.S. diplomacy that provided comedian Victor Moore with one of his meatiest roles. The show is best remembered today for introducing Broadway to the show-stopping charms of Mary Martin, who introduced "My Heart Belongs to Daddy," Cole Porter's hymn for a loyal sugar baby. Moore's part was that of mild-mannered Alonzo P. "Stinky" Goodhue, who is unwillingly appointed ambassador to the Soviet Union because his ambitious wife has contributed handsomely to President Roosevelt's re-election campaign. With the aid of foreign correspondent Buckley Joyce Thomas (William Gaxton), Goodhue does everything he can to be recalled, but all of his blunders only succeed in making him a hero. Finally he introduces a plan to ensure world peace—which of course no one wants. Stinky is soon happily on his way back to Kansas.

MISS SAIGON

MUSIC: Claude-Michel Schönberg
LYRICS: Richard Maltby, Jr. and Alain Boublil
DIRECTOR: Nicholas Hytner
MUSICAL STAGING: Bob Avian
OPENED: 9/20/89, London; 4,264 performances
　　　　　　 4/11/91, New York; still running as of 7/1/2000

As follow-up to their hit *Les Misérables*, Boublil and Schönberg boldly chose to update and transpose the Belasco/Puccini tale of the tragic Madame Butterfly to the Vietnam War of the 1970s. Instead of a sailor in 19th century Japan, the story now deals with a Marine living through the fall of Saigon at the end of the war. As in the original story, there is a hot romance between the soldier and a native girl, maybe even love, but then the lovers are torn apart by history. *Miss Saigon* follows the soldier (Chris) as he attempts to build a civilian life back home—with an American wife. Meanwhile, the girl, Kim, is left to raise their half-American child in Communist Vietnam, all the while plotting to escape and rejoin her man, whom she assumes is waiting for her. The writers cite a news photograph of a woman giving up her child to an American G.I. as the genesis of the idea. The production is noted for a life-size helicopter that descends on the stage and whisks Chris, but not Kim, away as the enemy conquers the city. "I'd Give My Life for You" is Kim's desperate lullabye to her baby.

PARADE

MUSIC AND LYRICS: Jason Robert Brown
BOOK: Alfred Uhry
DIRECTOR: Harold Prince
CHOREOGRAPHER: Patricia Birch
OPENED: 12/17/98, New York, for a run of 84 performances

The musical that opened at New York's Lincoln Center got mostly negative reviews for its relentlessly downbeat subject matter: the true story of Leo Frank, a Jewish factory manager accused of—and lynched for—the murder of Mary Phagan, an underage female worker, in 1913 Atlanta. But the sterling cast album released a few months later helped build a cult of devoted fans for this short-run musical, which went on to win the 1999 Tony Awards for Best Score and Best Book of a Musical. During Leo's trial the dead girl's mother testifies about her impoverished upbringing, which turns into "My Child Will Forgive Me," a heartbreaking apology to the daughter's spirit for a childhood that put her in such fatal danger. Later, a reporter approaches Leo's wife Lucille for some insight into the crime and the accused. Lucille replies with "You Don't Know This Man," in which she affirms her faith in the decency and honesty of her husband, and bitterly accuses the reporter of distorting his life.

RUTHLESS

MUSIC: Marvin Laird
BOOK, LYRICS AND DIRECTION: Joel Paley
OPENED: 5/6/92, New York, a run of 302 performances

This campy Off-Broadway musical is the story of 8-year-old *enfant terrible* Tina Denmark, who is willing to do anything, *anything*, to be a star. Driven by a ferocious stage mother, Tina claws her way through the seamy underside of show business—adding no small measure of seaminess of her own. The show spoofs every cliché of show business in every backstage film and stage musical ever. In the comedy number "Teaching Third Grade," Tina's teacher tries to persuade Tina's mom that there's more to life than being a star. But she's not very convincing, even to herself.

ST. LOUIS WOMAN

MUSIC: Harold Arlen
LYRICS: Johnny Mercer
BOOK: Arna Bontemps and Countee Cullen
DIRECTOR: Rouben Mamoulian
CHOREOGRAPHER: Charles Walters
OPENED: 3/30/46, New York; a run of 113 performances

St. Louis Woman, based on Arna Bontemps novel, *God Sends Sunday*, was something of a non-operatic *Porgy and Bess*. Set in 1898, it tells of a fickle St. Louis woman, Della Green, who is first the girlfriend of saloon-keeper Bigelow Brown, then falls for Li'l Augie, a jockey with an incredible winning streak. Before Brown is killed by a rejected lover, he puts a curse on Li'l Augie which ends the winning steak and cools Della's affection. The lovers are, however, reunited for the final singing of their impassioned duet, "Come Rain or Come Shine." In 1959, a revised version of *St. Louis Woman*, relocated to New Orleans and retitled *Free and Easy*, was performed in Amsterdam and Paris. "I Had Myself a True Love" is a rarely heard ballad from the composer of "Over the Rainbow."

SIDE SHOW

MUSIC: Henry Krieger
LYRICS AND BOOK: Bill Russell
DIRECTOR AND CHOREOGRAPHER: Robert Longbottom
OPENED: 10/16/97, New York; a run of 91 performances

She's Daisy; she's Violet. They're Siamese twins. That's the offbeat story of this fictionalized biography of real-life joined-at-the-hip twins Daisy and Violet Hilton, who climbed from carnival freak show through vaudeville to the Ziegfeld Follies in the early decades of the 20th century. The musical concentrates on their doomed romance with the two men who act as their coach and agent, but who ultimately can't get over what they see as the sisters' deformity. The show attracted a small but devoted cult that was unable to keep the show running more than three months. Stars Emily Skinner and Alice Ripley, who suggested their conjoined state simply by standing side by side and pressing together one hip each, have appeared together repeatedly since, including *James Joyce's The Dead (2000)*. The composer of *Dreamgirls* supplied the sisters with another powerhouse Act I finale, "Who Will Love Me As I Am?" which recalls his "And I Am Telling You I'm Not Going."

SONG AND DANCE

MUSIC: Andrew Lloyd Webber
LYRICS: Don Black, Richard Maltby Jr.
ADAPTATION: Richard Maltby Jr.
DIRECTOR: Richard Maltby Jr.
CHOREOGRAPHER: Peter Martins
OPENED: 9/18/85, New York; a run of 474 performances

The Dance of the title originated in 1979 when Andrew Lloyd Webber composed a set of variations on Paganini's A minor Capriccio that seemed to him to be perfect for a ballet. The *Song* originated a year later with a one-woman television show, *Tell Me on a Sunday*, which consisted entirely of musical pieces. Two years after that, both works were presented together in London as a full evening's entertainment, now connected with a bit of plot. In New York, this unconventional package won high praise for Bernadette Peters, whose task in Act I was to create, without dialogue or other actors, the character of a free-spirited English girl who has dalliances in America with four men. "Let Me Finish" is a phone conversation in which she tries to explain the things that are going wrong in her life. "Third Letter Home" offers more worldly-wise advice.

SONGS FOR A NEW WORLD

MUSIC AND LYRICS: Jason Robert Brown
DIRECTOR: Daisy Prince
CHOREOGRAPHER: Michael Arnold
OPENED: 10/26/95, New York; a run of 27 performances

In 1994, Daisy Prince, daughter of Broadway legend Harold Prince, went to hear a 24-year-old Greenwich Village coffee-house pianist named Jason Robert Brown play some of his original compositions. When she heard he was working on a concert evening of songs that played like offbeat short stories, a collaboration and a friendship were born. Titled *Songs for a New World*, the piece was developed at a summer festival Livent Inc. sponsored in Toronto, and the piece made its Off-Broadway bow Oct. 25, 1995. Musically distinctive and precocious, the songs look at contemporary life from highly unusual angles. In "Stars and the Moon," a woman regrets that she's been offered those two commodities by a series of idealistic, worshipping men, but she's always turned them down in favor of safer, more earthly pleasures. Not bad for a composer who had just turned 25. Brown's next project, *Parade*, was directed by Prince pere on Broadway in 1998, and won him the 1999 Tony Award for Best Score at age 29.

SOUTH PACIFIC

MUSIC: Richard Rodgers
LYRICS: Oscar Hammerstein II
BOOK: Oscar Hammerstein II and Joshua Logan
DIRECTOR: Joshua Logan
OPENED: 4/7/49, New York; a run of 1,925 performances

South Pacific had the second longest Broadway run of the nine musicals with songs by Richard Rodgers and Oscar Hammerstein II. Director Joshua Logan first urged the partners to adapt a short story, "Fo' Dolla," contained in James Michener's book about World War II, *Tales of the South Pacific*. Rodgers and Hammerstein, however, felt that the story—about Lt. Joe Cable's tender romance with Liat, a Polynesian girl—was a bit too much like *Madame Butterfly*, and they suggested that another story in the collection, "Our Heroine," should provide the main plot. This one was about the unlikely attraction between Nellie Forbush, a naive Navy nurse from Little Rock, and Emile de Becque, a sophisticated French planter living on a Pacific island. The tales were combined by having Cable and de Becque go on a dangerous mission together behind Japanese lines. Coming just a few years after the war, and featuring several veterans in the cast, the show was enormously resonant with 1949 audiences. But there has not so far been a major Broadway revival. Perhaps because of its daring (for the time) theme of the evils of racial prejudice, it was also the second musical to be awarded the prestigious Pulitzer Prize for Drama. This production was the first of two musicals (the other was *The Sound of Music*) in which Mary Martin, who played Nellie, was seen as a Rodgers and Hammerstein heroine. It also marked the Broadway debut of famed Metropolitan Opera basso, Ezio Pinza, who played de Becque. Mitzi Gaynor and Rossano Brazzi starred in 20th Century-Fox's 1958 film version, also directed by Logan. In a variety show for the troops, Nellie dresses in sailor drag and sings "Honey Bun," a hot-blooded ode to the charms of a pretty girl that any sailor could appreciate, full of 1940s-era turns of speech.

SUNSET BOULEVARD

MUSIC: Andrew Lloyd Webber
LYRICS AND BOOK: Don Black and Christopher Hampton
DIRECTOR: Trevor Nunn
CHOREOGRAPHER: Bob Avian
OPENED: 11/17/94, New York; a run of 977 performances

Based on the 1950 Billy Wilder film, *Sunset Boulevard* provided Broadway and the West End with one of the great diva vehicles ever. Dealing with a tortured woman whose advancing age leads to rejection and madness, this musical shows the degenerate aftereffects of Hollywood stardom in all their gothic glory. The show premiered in London in 1993 with Patti LuPone as the former silent screen star Norma Desmond who is desperate to make a comeback (though she loathes that word). After several lawsuits, the Broadway role went to Glenn Close, who had played the role in Los Angeles. The story involves handsome young screenwriter Joe Gillis who stumbles into Norma Desmond's life. She falls in love with him, and he accepts her lavish attention. Miss Desmond has a pathetic plan to return to the screen with her own hopelessly overwritten adaptation of Salome. She thrills when the studio requests a meeting. But she's then crushed when she learns they don't want her—they want her vintage car, as an antique prop. Her life and sanity quickly fly apart, with tragic consequences for all. The score includes two juicy, pull-out-the-stops soliloquies for Norma. She tells Joe about the magical power she had over audiences in "With One Look." "As If We Never Said Goodbye" captures her swirl of memory and emotion as she arrives at the movie studio after an absence of decades.

WORKING

MUSIC AND LYRICS: Stephen Schwartz, Craig Carnelia, James Taylor, Micki Grant,
Mary Rodgers and Susan Birkenhead
BOOK AND DIRECTION: Stephen Schwartz
CHOREOGRAPHER: Onna White
OPENED: 5/14/78, New York; a run of 25 performances

Adapted from Studs Terkel's Pulitzer-winning book of interviews with all walks of working men and women, this revue-type musical follows a typical workday around the clock. We meet a waitress, a fireman, a builder, a teacher, a retiree, a cleaning lady, a parking lot attendant, a millworker, and many more, offering a cross-section of attitudes about the kind of work people do and why they do it. Some of their stories are funny, some stoic, some deeply touching. As Terkel put it, "Its theme is about a search for daily meaning as well as daily bread, for recognition as well as cash." To express its eclectic characters, *Working* had a score by an assortment of writers with a variety of distinctive styles and ethnic backgrounds. In the wake of *A Chorus Line*, the doors seemed open for this group-character type of show. But its quick failure was devastating to Schwartz, who had written three of the longest-running musicals of the 1970s, *Pippin*, *Godspell* and *The Magic Show*. So far, Schwartz has never returned to Broadway as a composer. On April 14, 1982, a TV version was first aired over the Public Broadcasting System. In Craig Carnelia's haunting "Just a Housewife," a woman struggles to understand why a job that was good enough for her mother suddenly seems so unfashionable and meaningless—to everyone but her.

YOU'RE A GOOD MAN, CHARLIE BROWN

MUSIC, LYRICS AND BOOK: Charles Gesner; Andrew Lippa added songs for the Broadway revival
DIRECTOR: Joseph Hardy
CHOREOGRAPHER: Patricia Birch
OPENED: 3/7/67, New York; a run of 1,597 performances

With Charles Schultz's appealing comic strip "Peanuts" as a general inspiration, Clark Gesner created a musical out of events in "a day made up of little moments picked from all the days of Charlie Brown, from Valentine's Day to the baseball season, from wild optimism to utter despair, all mixed with the lives of his friends (both human and non-human) and strung together on the string of a single day, from bright uncertain morning to hopeful starlit evening." Whew! For the 1997 Broadway revival, Andrew Lippa wrote two new numbers, including, "My New Philosophy" for Sally, which became the standout number of the show. Sally has just gotten a D- at school, and is struggling to bounce back.

YOU CAN'T GET A MAN WITH A GUN

from the stage production *Annie Get Your Gun*

Words and Music by
IRVING BERLIN

THEY SAY IT'S WONDERFUL

from the stage production *Annie Get Your Gun*

Words and Music by
IRVING BERLIN

Slowly, with expression

VERSE

ANNIE:

Ru - mors fly and you can't tell where they start, _____

'Spec - 'lly when it con - cerns a per - son's heart, _____

I've heard tales that could set my heart a - glow, _____

Wish I knew if the things I heard are so.

CHORUS

a tempo

They say that fall-ing in love is won - der-ful, _____ It's

won - der-ful _____ so they say. _____

And with a moon up a-bove it's won - der-ful, _____ It's

won - der - ful _____ so they tell me. _____ I

can't re - call who said it, I know I nev - er read it, I

on - ly know they tell me that love is grand, and,

The thing that's known as ro-mance is won - der-ful, won - der-ful,

GORGEOUS

from *The Apple Tree*

Words and Music by JERRY BOCK
and SHELDON HARNICK

sign me. My cup run - neth o - ver.

Who ev - er saw such a com-plete wow?!

No-bod - y could say no to me now! ___

No one ___

A CHANGE IN ME

from Walt Disney's *Beauty and the Beast:*
The Broadway Musical

Music by ALAN MENKEN
Lyrics by TIM RICE

There's been a change in me,
A kind of mov-ing on, Though what I used to be
I still de-pend up-on. For now I re-a-lize

* *Original Broadway key: G♭*

SO WHAT?
from the musical *Cabaret*

Words by FRED EBB
Music by JOHN KANDER

FRÄULEIN SCHNEIDER:
You say fifty marks,
I say one hundred marks, a -

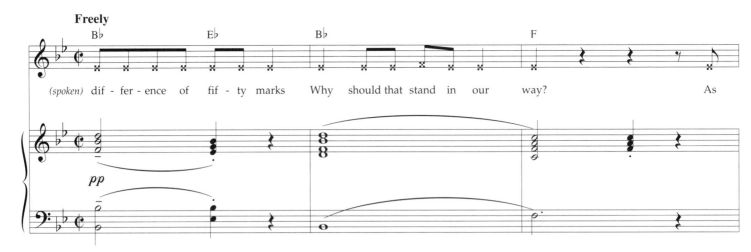

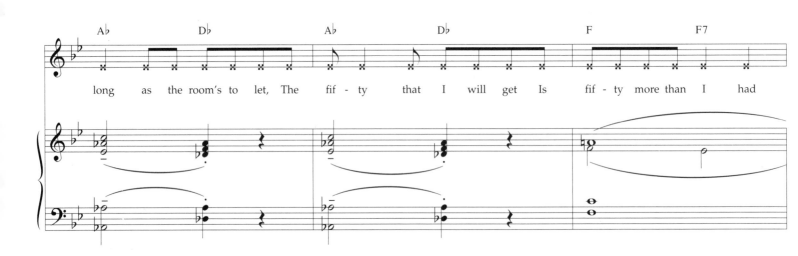

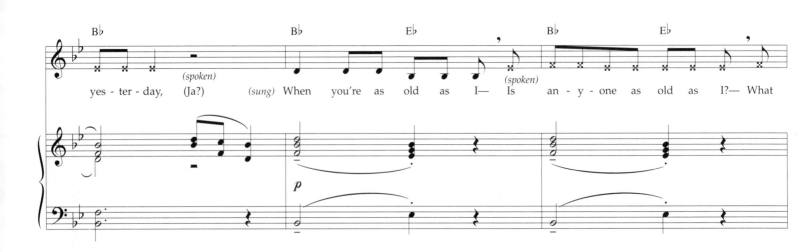

Allegretto - con pesante

Marziale

MEIN HERR
from the musical *Cabaret*

Words by FRED EBB
Music by JOHN KANDER

48

50

MAYBE THIS TIME
from the musical *Cabaret*

Words by FRED EBB
Music by JOHN KANDER

In the 1998 Broadway Revival this final section was performed in an understated, soft way.

WHEN YOU'RE GOOD TO MAMA

from *Chicago*

Words by FRED EBB
Music by JOHN KANDER

MARY:

Ask an-y of the chick-ies in my pen. They'll tell you I'm the big-gest moth-er hen. I love them all and all of them love me Be-cause the sys-tem works, the sys-tem called rec-i-proc-i-ty!

Got a lit-tle mot - to, al - ways sees me through,___
If you want my gra - vy, pep - per my ra - gout,___

When you're good to Ma - ma, Ma - ma's good to you.___
Spice it up for Ma - ma, She'll get hot for you.___

There's a lot of fa - vors I'm pre - pared to do.___
When they pass that bas - ket folks con - trib - ute to.___

CLASS
from *Chicago*

Words by FRED EBB
Music by JOHN KANDER

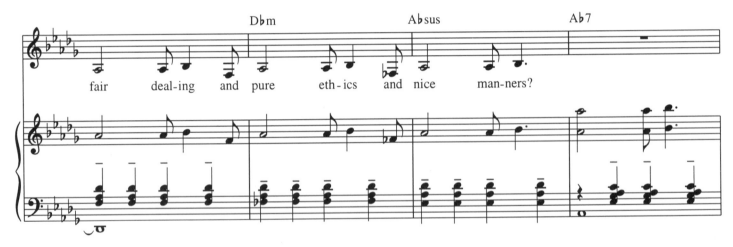

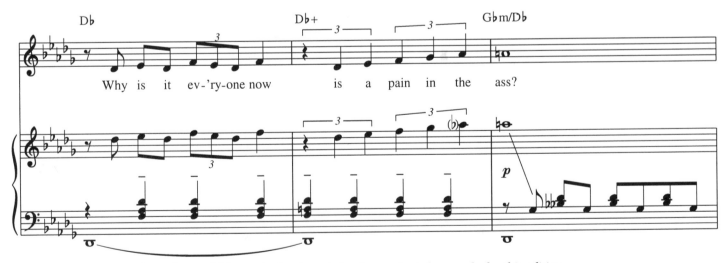

This number is a duet for Velma and Matron in the show; it has been adapted as a solo for this edition.

Now no one e-ven says "oops" when they're pass-ing their gas.

What ev - er hap - pened to class? Class!
(or spoken)

Ah, _____ there ain't no gen - tle - men who's fit for an - y use, _____ and an - y

girl - 'd touch your pri-vates for a deuce. _____ And e - ven kids - 'll kick your shins and give ya

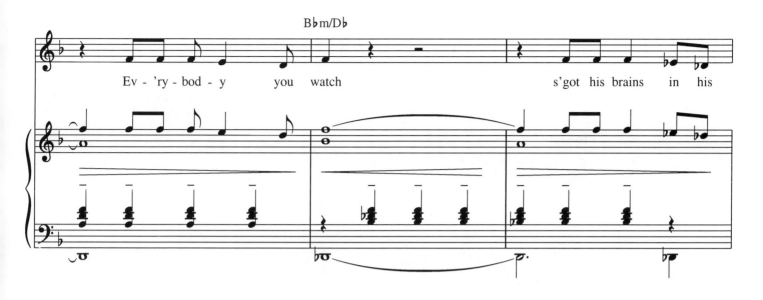

Ev - 'ry - bod - y you watch s'got his brains in his

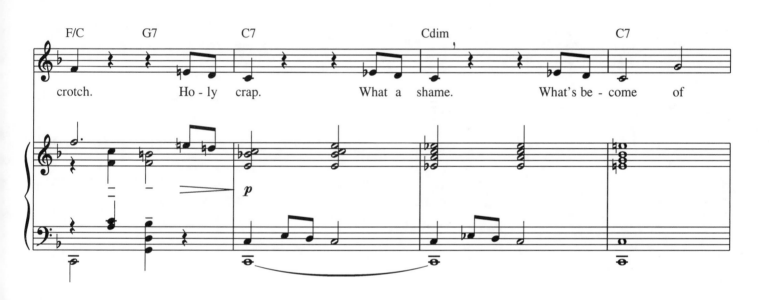

crotch. Ho - ly crap. What a shame. What's be - come of

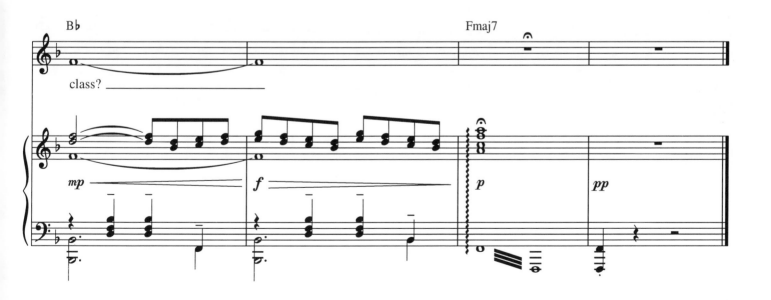

class? _____

NOTHING
from *A Chorus Line*

Words by EDWARD KLEBAN
Music by MARVIN HAMLISCH

Easy 2 - Rock feel

DIANA:

Spoken:

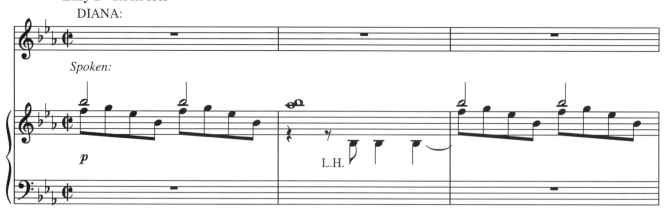

I mean, I was dying to be a serious actress. Anyway it's the first day of acting class and we're in the

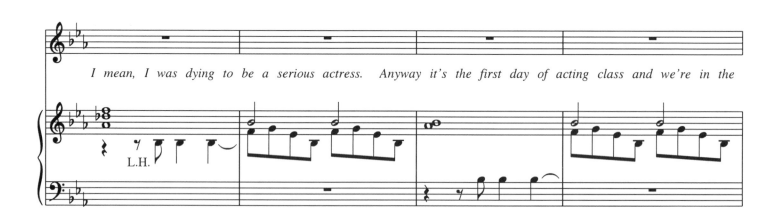

auditorium and the teacher, Mister Karp, puts us up on the stage with our legs around everybody, one in back of

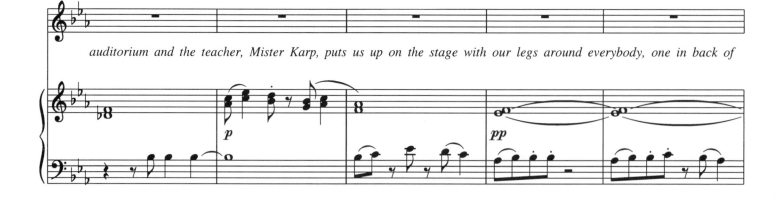

the other, and he says: O.K., we're gonna do improvisations. Now, you're on a bobsled

rall.

and it's snowing out. And it's cold . . . O.K., go!

Ev-'ry-day for a week we would try to

feel   the mo - tion,   feel   the mo - tion

bot-tom of my soul and I tried, _____ I tried.

Spoken: Everyone is going: "Woosh... I feel the snow, I feel the cold...the air." And Mr. Karp

turns to me and says: "O.K. Morales, what did you feel?" *Sung:* And I said, "Noth-ing, __

Vamp under dialogue

I'm feel - ing noth-ing," __ and he says, "Noth-ing __ could

72

get a girl trans - ferred!" They all felt some-thing, __

but I felt noth - ing __ ex - cept the

feel - ing that this bull - shit was ab - surd! *Spoken: But I said to myself:*

"Hey!, it's only the first week. Maybe it's genetic. They don't have bob sleds in San Juan."

74

"Noth-ing!"_ And Karp al - lowed it, which real - ly makes me

burn. They were so help - ful. They called me

hope - less. Un - til I real - ly did - n't know where else to

turn! *Spoken: And Karp kept saying:* "*Morales, I think you should transfer to girls' high.*"

help me feel it. Pret-ty please!" And a

voice from down at the bot-tom of my soul came up to the top of my head. And the

voice from down at the bot-tom of my soul, here is what it

said: "This man is noth-ing! This course is

noth - ing! __ If you want some - thing, go

find a bet - ter class. And when you

find one, you'll be an act - ress."

And I as - sure you that's what fi - n'lly came to pass.

Ad lib.

Six months lat-er I heard that Karp had died.____

And I dug right down to the bot-tom of my soul....

Slowly

and cried,_____ 'cause I felt. . .

Tempo I

noth - ing.____

THE LADIES WHO LUNCH

from *Company*

Music and Lyrics by
STEPHEN SONDHEIM

Molto rubato

JOANNE:

Spoken: I'd like to propose a toast. Here's to the la - dies who lunch— Ev - 'ry - bod - y

laugh.   Loung-ing in their caf-tans and plan - ning a brunch On their own be -

half. _____   Off to the gym, Then to a fit - ting,

Claim-ing they're fat, _____

And look-ing grim 'Cause they've been sit-ting

choos-ing a hat. ___ *Spoken: Does anyone still wear a hat?*

Slow Bossa Nova

rit.

p

I'll drink to that.

Here's to the girls __ who stay smart. Are-n't they a gas?

Rush-ing to their class-es in op - ti - cal art, ___ Wish-ing it would

pass.

An-oth-er long, ex - haust-ing day. _

An - oth - er thou - sand dol - lars. _ A mat - i - nee: A

Pin - ter play, _ Per-haps a piece of Mah - ler's. _____ I'll drink to

that—

And one for Mah-ler.

Here's to the girls __ who play wife. __ Are-n't they too

much? _____ Keep-ing house, but clutch-ing a cop - y of *Life* __

Just to keep in touch.

The

here's to the girls __ who just watch. __ Are-n't they the best?

When they get de-pressed, it's a bot - tle of Scotch __ Plus a lit - tle

jest. An-oth-er chance to dis-ap - prove. __

An - oth - er bril - liant zin - ger. __ An - oth - er rea - son

(Scream)

not to move, __ An - oth - er vod - ka sting - er. Aaah _____

_____ I'll drink to that. So

here's to the girls __ on the go, __ Ev - 'ry - bod - y tries.

Look in - to their eyes and you'll see __ what they know: __ Ev - 'ry - bod - y

HEADS OR TAILS

from *Cowgirls*

Written by MARY MURFITT

DON'T CALL ME TRAILER TRASH

from *Cowgirls*

Written by MARY MURFITT

Steadily

look at all them pic - tures in the mag - a - zines___ where they
You can al - ways keep me down on the farm 'cause I've

show you all the mod - els in de - sign - er jeans.
al - ways liked a man with a half tan arm.

ADVENTURE

from *Do Re Mi*

Words by BETTY COMDEN and ADOLPH GREEN
Music by JULE STYNE

Spoken before the song:
Should I have married Seymour Brilkin?

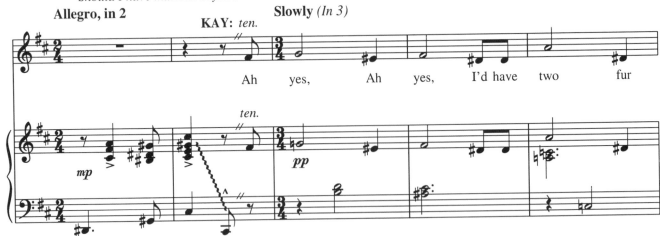

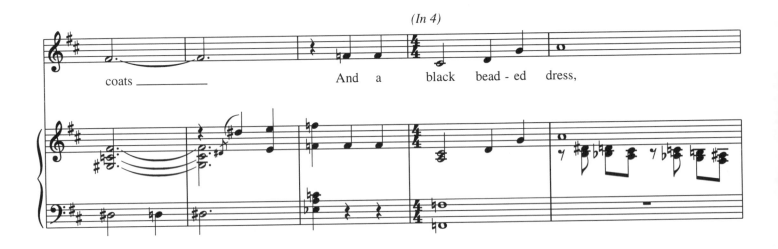

The introduction to the song, edited out of this edition, is sung by Hubie. Other adaptations have been made for this solo edition.

ie. _____ My life is a

ball, it's the "Per - ils of Paul - ine" with

my name up on the mar - quee! _____

It's ad - ven - ture for me!

hors - es. _____ *Spoken: Should I have married Sheldon Miller?* So

why is it I'm told The hors - y Miss - us

poco a poco rit.

Mil - ler is jeal - ous of me? _____ 'Cause I've got ad -

(In 4) *ten.* 3 *rall.* *ten.* *ten.*

Fast (In 4)

ven - ture, _____ Ad - ven - ture, _____

mf

The place that we stay is in

Far Rock - a - way, With a heav - en - ly

view of the sea. _____ But the

bill soon ar - rives, so we run for our

lives, Out the win - dow, by dark, we con -

A little faster

tin - ue our lark. We drop to the

streets on a lad - der of sheets, It's an

un - ob - served drop, all ex - cept for one

cop. We flee, hand in hand, down the damp mid - night sand, By a great piece of luck there's the back of a truck. It bumps us to town, I'm still in my night - gown. Well, the

AH, BUT UNDERNEATH

from *Follies*

Words and Music by
STEPHEN SONDHEIM

UPTOWN, DOWNTOWN
from *Follies*

Words and Music by
STEPHEN SONDHEIM

With a swing (♩.=124)

Now this is the

tale of a dame known as Har-ri-et, _____ Who climbed to the top of the heap _____ from the

bot-tom. _____ A beau-ti-ful life was her aim and, to var-y it, _____ She want-ed the

sun and the moon, _ And she got 'em. _____ She is-n't the least ex - haust - ed

from her _ climb, _ But she does look back from time to _ time. _ And the

sub - ject of this ev - 'ning's _ quiz _ Is who she was and

who she _ is. _

chelle. _____ Up - town, _____

_____ she's got the Van - der - bilt clans. _

Down - town, _____ She's with the side - walk Ce - zannes. _

Hy - phen - at - ed Har - ri - et, The nou - veau from New_ Ro -

She's two of the most mis' - ra -

- ble girls in town.

CAN YOU FIND IT IN YOUR HEART?

from the Broadway musical *Footloose*

Words by DEAN PITCHFORD
Music by TOM SNOW

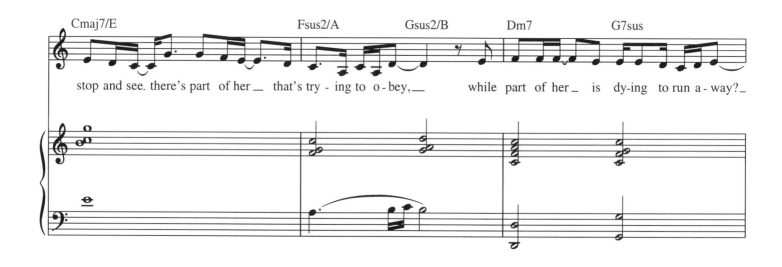

DON'T RAIN ON MY PARADE

from *Funny Girl*

Words by BOB MERRILL
Music by JULE STYNE

spill, It's me and not you. Who told __ you you're al - lowed to rain on my pa -

rade?

I'll march my band out, ___

I'll beat my drum.

And if I'm

fanned out, ___

Your turn at bat, sir, ___

At

got - ta try once, On - ly can die once. Right, sir? __ Ooh, love is juic - y, Juic-

y and you see I got - ta have my bite sir! __ Get read - y for me, __

__ love, 'Cause I'm a "com - er." I sim - ply got - ta __ march 'Cause I'm a drum-mer.

Don't bring __ a - round a __ cloud To rain on my pa - rade. __

132

I'm gon-na live and live now! Get what I want I know

how. One roll for the whole she - bang! One throw, that bell will go

clang! Eye on the tar-get and wham! One shot, one gun shot and

Slowly

bam! Hey, Mist - ter Arn - stein, Here I am! _____

BUT NOT FOR ME

from *Girl Crazy*

Music and Lyrics by GEORGE GERSHWIN
and IRA GERSHWIN

Note: While not the original key, this key will be vocally friendly to most mezzos.

EVERYTHING'S COMING UP ROSES

from *Gypsy*

Words by STEPHEN SONDHEIM
Music by JULE STYNE

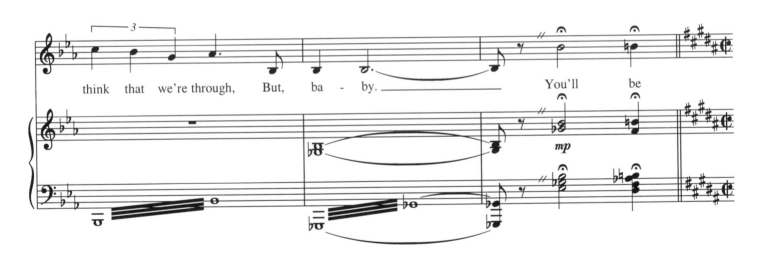

Slowly (♩=60)

You can do it, All you need is a hand. We can

do it, Mom-ma is gon-na see to it! Cur-tain

up! Light the lights! We got

noth-ing to hit but the heights! I can

ROSE'S TURN

from *Gypsy*

Words by STEPHEN SONDHEIM
Music by JULE STYNE

You like it? Well, I

got it. Some peo - ple got it and

make it pay. __ Some __ peo - ple can't e - ven give it a - way! __

This peo - ple's got it And this peo - ple's __ spread - in' it a - round. __

Hold your hats and hal - le - lu - jah, Mom - ma's gon - na show it to ya.

Thanks a lot and out __ with the gar - bage. They take bows and you're __ bat - tin' ze - ro!

I had a dream. __ I

dreamed it for you, June. __ It

MISS MARMELSTEIN

from *I Can Get It for You Wholesale*

Words and Music by
HAROLD ROME

ALWAYS A BRIDESMAID

from *I Love You, You're Perfect, Now Change*

Lyrics by JOE DiPIETRO
Music by JIMMY ROBERTS

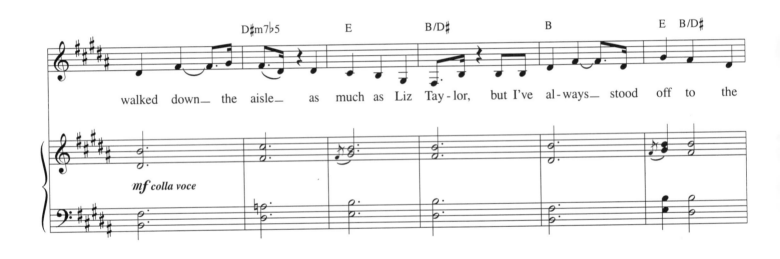

NOTHING REALLY HAPPENED

from the Broadway musical *Is There Life After High School?*

Music and Lyric by
CRAIG CARNELIA

SOMEONE LIKE YOU

from *Jekyll & Hyde*

Words by LESLIE BRICUSSE
Music by FRANK WILDHORN

A NEW LIFE

from *Jekyll & Hyde*

Words by LESLIE BRICUSSE
Music by FRANK WILDHORN

LUCY:

A new life, what I would-n't give to have a

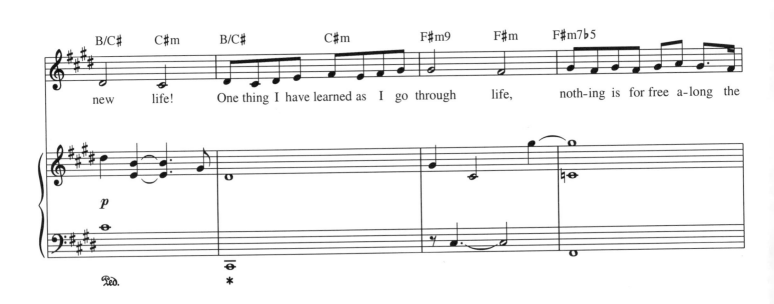

new life! One thing I have learned as I go through life, noth-ing is for free a-long the

MY HEART BELONGS TO DADDY

from *Leave It to Me*

Words and Music by
COLE PORTER

I'D GIVE MY LIFE FOR YOU

from *Miss Saigon*

Music by CLAUDE-MICHEL SCHÖNBERG
Lyrics by RICHARD MALTBY JR. and ALAIN BOUBLIL
Adapted from original French Lyrics by ALAIN BOUBLIL

Andante appassionata

Not too slow
KIM:

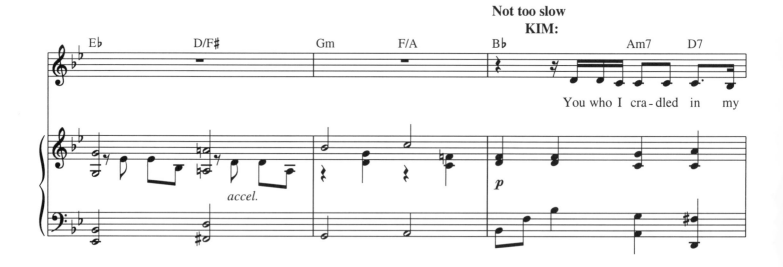

You who I cra-dled in my

arms. You ask-ing ___ as lit-tle as you can. ___

I've tast-ed love be-yond all fear. And you should know it's love that

brought you here.— And in one per-fect night when the stars burned like new, I knew what I must

do. I'll give you __ a mil-lion things I'll nev-er own, I'll

give you __ a world to con-quer when you're grown.

Più mosso, appassionata

MY CHILD WILL FORGIVE ME

from *Parade*

Music and Lyrics by
JASON ROBERT BROWN

MRS. PHAGAN:

My child will for-give me for

rais - in' her poor, and for tak - in' her out of the school.

My child will for-give me for not do - in' more ___ to pro -

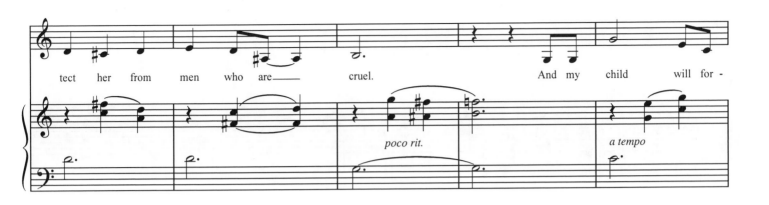

tect her from men who are____ cruel. And my child will for-

poco rit.   *a tempo*

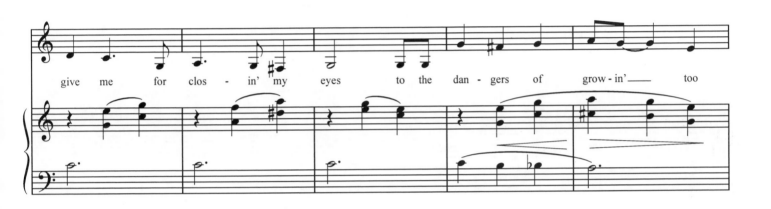

give me for clos - in' my eyes to the dan - gers of grow - in'____ too

fast. My____ child will for - give me with tears in her

pp

eyes when we're re - u - nit - ed at last.____

rit.   *mp a tempo*

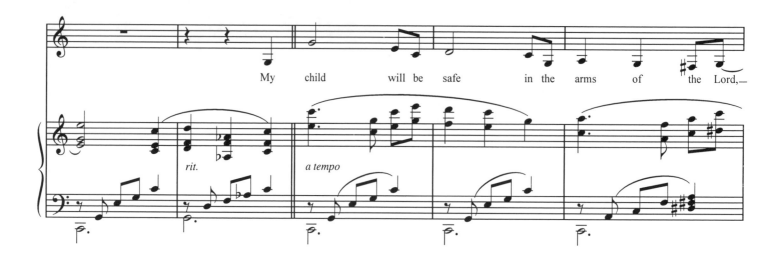

My child will be safe in the arms of the Lord,—

and as pure as the day—— of her—— birth. My

child will be co-zied and blessed and a-dored as she

nev - er could be here on Earth. And my

child will be watch - in' me, giv - in' me faith in a

arpeggiated quickly, ad lib.
colla voce

fu - ture that's gold - en and new. My Mar - y will

rall.

p

teach me to o - pen my heart, and so I for - give you, Jew.

rall.

YOU DON'T KNOW THIS MAN
from *Parade*

Music and Lyrics by
JASON ROBERT BROWN

You don't know this man.

You don't e - ven try. When a man writes his

moth - er ev - 'ry Sun - day, pays his bills be - fore they're due, works so hard to feed his fam - 'ly, there's your

mur - der - er for you! And you stand here spit - ting words that you know aren't true. Then

TEACHING THIRD GRADE

from *Ruthless*

Lyric by JOEL PALEY
Music by MARVIN LAIRD

I HAD MYSELF A TRUE LOVE

from *St. Louis Woman*

Words by JOHNNY MERCER
Music by HAROLD ARLEN

WHO WILL LOVE ME AS I AM?

from *Side Show*

Words by BILL RUSSELL
Music by HENRY KRIEGER

Ballad

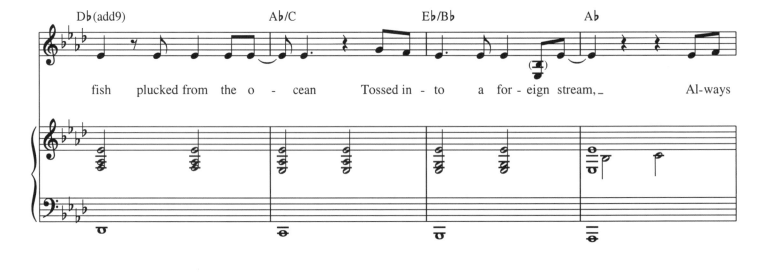

Daisy and Violet sing this number as a duet in the show; adapted as a solo for this edition.

*optional duet part

LET ME FINISH
from *Song & Dance*

Words by DON BLACK
Music by ANDREW LLOYD WEBBER

THIRD LETTER HOME

from *Song & Dance*

Words by DON BLACK
Music by ANDREW LLOYD WEBBER

HONEY BUN

from *South Pacific*

Lyrics by OSCAR HAMMERSTEIN II
Music by RICHARD RODGERS

Ev-'ry inch is packed with dy - na - mite! _____ Her

hair is blonde and curl - y, Her curls are hur - ly bur - ly. Her

lips are pips!_ I call her hips: _ "Twirl - y" __ and "Whirl - y."__

She's my ba - by, I'm her pap!_ I'm her boo - by, she's my trap!_

AS IF WE NEVER SAID GOODBYE

from *Sunset Boulevard*

Music by ANDREW LLOYD WEBBER
Lyrics by DON BLACK and CHRISTOPHER HAMPTON,
with contributions by AMY POWERS

Moderato

NORMA

colla voce

I don't know why I'm fright-ened ___ I know my way a-round here. ___ The card-board trees, the paint-ed seas, ___ the sound here. ___ Yes, a world to re-dis-cov-er, ___ but I'm not in a-ny hur-ry, ___ and I need a mo-ment. The whis-pered con-ver-sa-tions ___ in

WITH ONE LOOK
from *Sunset Boulevard*

Music by ANDREW LLOYD WEBBER
Lyrics by DON BLACK and CHRISTOPHER HAMPTON,
with contributions by AMY POWERS

JUST A HOUSEWIFE
from the Broadway musical *Working*

Music and Lyric by
CRAIG CARNELIA

MY NEW PHILOSOPHY

from *You're a Good Man, Charlie Brown*

Words and Music by
ANDREW LIPPA

SALLY: *Spoken (before the vamp): "Why are you telling me?" (beat) I like it.*

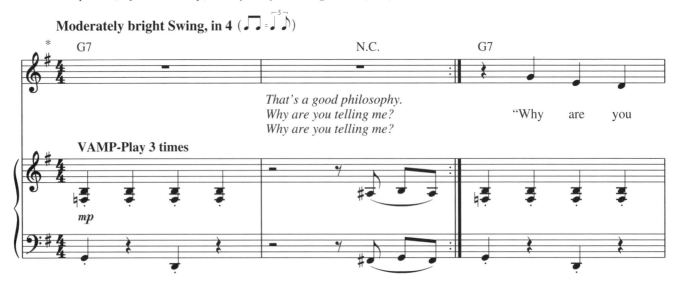

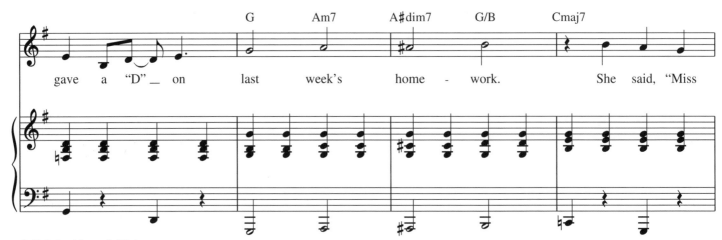

* *Original key: A Major*
The song is a duet for Sally and Schroeder. The composer created this solo edition for publication.

STARS AND THE MOON

from *Songs for a New World*

Music and Lyrics by
JASON ROBERT BROWN

Folk Rock, gentle (♩ = 60)

I met a man with-out a dol - lar to his name,— who— had no traits of an-y val - ue but his smile